To
My g[...]
Thanks for your words of wisdom and guidance. Much love and many prayers for your healing. God is able to do exceedingly above all things we could ask or imagine.

Much love
Dear One,
Cynthia

FORTY CONVERSATIONS
with
GOD

Dr. Cynthia D. Davis

WESTBOW
PRESS®
A DIVISION OF THOMAS NELSON
& ZONDERVAN

Copyright © 2021 Dr. Cynthia D. Davis.

All rights reserved. No part of this book may be used or reproduced by any means, graphic, electronic, or mechanical, including photocopying, recording, taping or by any information storage retrieval system without the written permission of the author except in the case of brief quotations embodied in critical articles and reviews.

WestBow Press books may be ordered through booksellers or by contacting:

WestBow Press
A Division of Thomas Nelson & Zondervan
1663 Liberty Drive
Bloomington, IN 47403
www.westbowpress.com
844-714-3454

Because of the dynamic nature of the Internet, any web addresses or links contained in this book may have changed since publication and may no longer be valid. The views expressed in this work are solely those of the author and do not necessarily reflect the views of the publisher, and the publisher hereby disclaims any responsibility for them.

Any people depicted in stock imagery provided by Getty Images are models, and such images are being used for illustrative purposes only. Certain stock imagery © Getty Images.

Scripture quotations marked NRSV are from the New Revised Standard Version Bible, copyright © 1989 the Division of Christian Education of the National Council of the Churches of Christ in the United States of America. Used by permission. All rights reserved.

Scripture quotations marked CEB are taken from the Common English Bible. Copyright 2012 by Common English Bible and/or its suppliers. All rights reserved.

Scripture quotations marked MSG are taken from The Message. Copyright © 1993, 1994, 1995, 1996, 2000, 2001, 2002. Used by permission of NavPress Publishing Group.

Scripture quotations marked NIV are taken from The Holy Bible, New International Version®, NIV® Copyright © 1973, 1978, 1984, 2011 by Biblica, Inc.® Used by permission. All rights reserved worldwide.

ISBN: 978-1-6642-2981-5 (sc)
ISBN: 978-1-6642-2982-2 (hc)
ISBN: 978-1-6642-2983-9 (e)

Library of Congress Control Number: 2021906627

Print information available on the last page.

WestBow Press rev. date: 06/04/2021

Preface

These forty devotional prayers are a brief sample of conversations I have had with God in my spiritual journey. Sometimes I come giddy with excitement, thanksgiving and praise; sometimes overwhelmed and fearful; sometimes exhausted or troubled. However I have come, I am assured that I am heard even in the deep recesses of my heart.

I chose forty because of the number's biblical significance. For instance:

- Jesus was in the wilderness fasting forty days and forty nights. (Matthew 4:2)
- Solomon and David were kings for forty years each. (I Kings 11:42), (I Kings 2:11)
- The spies sent out by Moses were on their expedition for forty days. (Numbers 13:25)
- Caleb was forty years old when he went to spy out the land of Canaan. (Joshua 14:7)
- Goliath came out to taunt the armies of Israel for forty days. (I Samuel 17:16)
- Jesus was with the disciples forty days following his resurrection. (Acts 1:3)

- Eli, Othniel, Deborah, Gideon and Barak judged Israel for forty years. (I Samuel 4:18), (Judges 3:10-11), (Judges 5:1-31), (Judges 8:28)
- The Israelites wandered in the wilderness for forty years. (Numbers 32:13)
- Moses fasted for forty days and forty nights before receiving the Ten Commandments. (Exodus 34:28)
- Elijah fasted forty days and forty nights and was strengthened for the journey. (I Kings 19:8)
- Jonah warned Nineveh that in forty days, it was doomed for destruction. (Jonah 3:4)
- Ezekiel laid on his right side forty days symbolizing the punishment of Judah (Ezekiel 4:6)
- The Book of Freedom, Exodus, is forty chapters long.
- Lent is a defined time of forty days not counting Sunday's, where fasting, reflection and introspection are done leading to Easter.

As you can see, forty has quite a bit of significance in scripture. Forty represented a time of testing: testing the resolve and spirit of a person or people, testing through trials, sometimes by fire, the character, integrity, fortitude and tenacity of those called to lead. Forty represented a time of growth, renewal, contemplation and a time of evaluation.

What is your forty?

My prayer is that these forty days of praying and reflecting on the scriptures will be spiritually encouraging in your journey.

Some of these prayers are a result of praying as I read the lectionary readings for the upcoming Sunday. Some came about as I experienced the world around me as family and friends attempted to navigate uncertain health issues, natural disasters, and a variety of personal and corporate trauma. I prayed some prayers in worship. I prayed some prayers in small groups. Some I just prayed as I sought to hear a word from the Lord.

As you pray these prayers either alone or in community, what is God stirring in your heart? Sometimes people say they don't know how to pray. I assure them all they are doing is having a conversation. We can't hide anything from God. He knows when we are angry or frustrated and even trying to hide our secrets from him. Prayers are a way of acknowledging feelings and emotions we need clarity around in a safe and sacred space. Then, we wait and listen for a divine response.

Each time I pray these prayers, I feel incredibly close to God. I need the presence of the Holy Spirit to hold me more times than I can tell you. I need the healing presence for myself and for the many I love and for those I am asked to pray with and for. Sometimes when we are too distraught or overwhelmed and the words seem to have escaped our vocabulary, I pray these words will be a helpful resource for you.

Over the next forty days, I pray your prayer life will be filled with new images, a different perspective and insight into a pastor's heart. Let your holy imagination allows you to visualize the vastness of the God we serve.

I pray that each person who prays these prayers will find themselves at the foot of the throne of grace.

Acknowledgment

First, I give thanks and praise to almighty God for the opportunity to publicly share in writing some of my conversations. To God be the glory!

So thankful for Carey Chapel AME Church in Jamestown, my home church, which modeled the faithfulness and love of God until I went off to college and eventually moved away from home. For all the churches who nurtured me in the faith, including Palestine, White's Chapel, St. Andrew, and Howard Chapel AME Churches, I thank God for you. Centenary, Friendship, and Christ United Methodist Churches, along with the churches of the former McKendree District and the Mississippi River District of the United Methodist Church, who helped shape and inform my journey.

For the teachers who pushed and encouraged me: Mrs. Gwin, Mrs. Hayes, Mrs. Rice, Mrs. Johnson, Mrs. Fayne, Mr. Harris, Mr. King, Mr. Smith, Mr. Epps, and countless others.

To my great-grandparents and grandparents who were examples of the faith every day in word and deed and showed us it could be done. I give thanks for the loving support of my husband, Sonny, who has been a strong, steady witness of the faith, hopeful and attentive in prayer and inspirational and committed in his walk; to my son, Derrick, who had the gift of being prophetic and discerning from the day he was born and who has always been my number one cheerleader; to my parents, Amos Ezekiel and Dollie Ruth who faithfully stayed on their knees trusting God for answers and giving thanks for blessings, and my siblings who are also best friends for life, Marvin, Steven and Dorothy, AJ and Lourrie, Reggie, Jackie, Chris, and Cheryl for their love and support as they sometimes walked with me through the valley of the shadow of death; and to Gladys, Calandra, Carrel, Jocelyn, Melissa, Jalen, and Blake, our forever faithful prayer squad.

To my nieces and nephews, tender, warmhearted, and prayer warriors in their own right.

For the many friends who have been fellow sojourners over the years: Deborah, Vinnie, Laritha, Pearl, Marcella, Senethua, Jo Andrea, Peggy, Bernice, Sandra, Donna, Carolyn, Leigh Ann, Betty, and Vicki.

For each of you, named and unnamed, I give God thanks for your witness.

1

And after flogging Jesus, he handed him over to be crucified. (Matthew 27:26 NRSV)

How many times have we said "crucify him"? When we denied justice to the innocent, rights to the poor, sustenance to the widow, guidance to the orphan, shelter for the homeless, a word of kindness to the downtrodden, comfort for the grieving, necessities in disaster, and when we preferred property and politics over people. How many times have we grieved the Holy Spirit?

So today we pray, Lord Jesus, that you would hide us in the wounds of your side that we may see the pain of our sisters and brothers. Hide us in the wounds of your hands that we may serve those who still trust in your abundant mercy. Hide us in the wounds of your back, that we may help shoulder the pain of those whose load has grown weary. Hide us in your mercy that we may forgive those who have wounded our spirits and left our hearts broken. Hide us in your presence so that each day we may take up our cross and follow you.

It is in the name of the One who bore our sins and gives us eternal life, Jesus the Christ. Amen.

1. As I am praying this prayer, I am remembering …

   _____
   _____
   _____
   _____
   _____
   _____
   _____

2. How am I being called to respond to this prayer?

   _____
   _____
   _____
   _____
   _____
   _____
   _____

3. What challenges me?

   _____
   _____
   _____
   _____
   _____
   _____
   _____

2

And when he got into the boat, his disciples followed him. A windstorm arose on the sea, so great that the boat was being swamped by the waves; but he was asleep. And they went and woke him up, saying, "Lord, save us! We are perishing!" And he said to them, "Why are you afraid, you of little faith?" Then he got up and rebuked the winds and the sea; and there was a dead calm. (Matthew 8:23–26 NRSV)

Almighty God, we come to you this morning in the name of Jesus Christ of Nazareth, the storm calmer! We come in the midst of tornadic and political storms! The hurricane force winds are more than we can endure. We need you to calm the storms of our fears and the storms of anger and the storms of hatred and storms of violence! Please say to our storms, "Peace, be still!"

For those who live with struggles of mental illness or emotional and spiritual challenges of life, please speak peace to their storms! When our brothers and sisters are hearing voices and seeing things not there, when their brains feel like a coil of yarn unable to unwind itself, speak peace!

For those who are struggling with sickness in their bodies—nausea and vomiting are constant companions, lab reports are all outside of the normal ranges, CAT scans show masses and shadows, surgeries on the horizon, children sick, parents sick, frustrations with the system, insurance issues and conflicts—Lord, please speak peace to them!

Bills due. Taxes. Electric. Sewage and garbage. Mortgage and groceries. Lord Jesus, speak peace, for I am about to go under.

I will not give up or give in to what I can see. I am trusting in the one who calms the storms of life that I cannot see and who says to my storms, "Peace, be still!"

1. As I am praying this prayer, I am remembering …

2. How am I being called to respond to this prayer?

3. What challenges me?

3

There was not a needy person among them, for as many as owned lands or houses sold them and brought the proceeds of what was sold. (Acts 4:34 NRSV)

Holy God, we come this day to worship you from the very depths of our hearts and give thanks for more blessings than we can count. We are grateful to be in a community of faith as we lift our collective voices toward heaven. Nothing and no one can compare to you or your wonder-working miracles. Your tender mercy and outpouring of compassion for the least, the lost, and the left behind is evident every day. I see the light of your glory in my friends and in my community. Your limitless forgiveness bestowed upon us keeps us humble.

Help us to be witnesses of your steadfast love by loving our neighbors and welcoming the stranger through providing food for every family in need, health care for every sick person, availability of mental health services for all, tutoring for struggling children, companionship for the elderly, justice for the disenfranchised, and a place of acceptance where people can find you and themselves. Help us meet people where they struggle so we can be your representatives in the world as we struggle with them.

Let their names be a sweet-smelling fragrance to your nostrils and their circumstances be a call to action for us. Hear our prayers O' God!

1. As I am praying this prayer, I am remembering …

   _____
   _____
   _____
   _____
   _____
   _____
   _____

2. How am I being called to respond to this prayer?

   _____
   _____
   _____
   _____
   _____
   _____
   _____

3. What challenges me?

   _____
   _____
   _____
   _____
   _____
   _____
   _____
   _____

4

I give you a new commandment, that you love one another. Just as I have loved you, you also should love one another. By this everyone will know that you are my disciples, if you have love for one another. (John 13:34–35 NRSV)

Great and Awesome Creator, help us to be witnesses of your compassion as we: visit those who need comfort, assurance, and care; as we carry the lamp of your glory arising out of drinking deeply from your overflowing well; as we faithfully live in the power of your inspired words; and as we serve your kingdom in the deep, abiding presence of your spirit within us. Help us to be generous and kind in our words and actions even with those whom we disagree. Help us to be witnesses in our demeanor so others will know we belong to you. Help us so that there is no deceit or arrogance in our persona, no lies on our lips, and no justification of wrong in our hearts. Help us to be witnesses and demonstrate your love and forgiveness toward others with grace-filled hearts and tangible actions. Help us to love all our brothers and sisters no matter the language, culture, gender identity, or nationality. No matter the side of town, the color of skin, the kinkiness or straightness of hair, or the light or darkness of their eyes. No matter their religious beliefs or no beliefs. Help us love even those who hate and despise us and do all manner of evil against us. Help us rise above hate. Help us love.

1. As I am praying this prayer, I am remembering …

2. How am I being called to respond to this prayer?

3. What challenges me?

5

Day by day, as they spent much time together in the temple, they broke bread at home and ate their food with glad and generous hearts, praising God and having the goodwill of all the people. And day by day the Lord added to their number those who were being saved. (Acts 2:46 NRSV)

Be present at our generous tables as we give thanks and pray for those whose tables are bare. Be with those whose money has dried up or whose jobs have been lost. Be with the communities of faith and goodwill who are feeding hungry children. There are pickups at churches and schools, so children won't have to go to bed hungry. Thanks be to God!

We give thanks for the generous donations that fill boxes to assist families as they line up around blocks to pick up needed food and supplies to feed and care for their families. Thank you, Lord Jesus, for potatoes and onions, apples and pears. Thank you for jars of peanut butter and cans of tuna. Thank you for the outpouring from people who don't know the names or where your children have come from but are moved with compassion to assist them.

Your Word is true; you do make highways in the desert! You do indeed strengthen our weak and feeble knees and hands. Our mouths shall forever praise you!

To the God who is bread when store shelves are empty, to the God who is cold bottled water during times of disaster, to the God who is a warm comforting blanket in the cold, we give you thanks and praise through Jesus Christ our Lord—amen!

1. As I am praying this prayer, I am remembering ...

   _____
   _____
   _____
   _____
   _____
   _____
   _____
   _____

2. How am I being called to respond to this prayer?

   _____
   _____
   _____
   _____
   _____
   _____
   _____
   _____

3. What challenges me?

   _____
   _____
   _____
   _____
   _____
   _____
   _____
   _____

6

In those days Hezekiah became sick and was at
the point of death ... Hezekiah wept bitterly ...
I have heard your prayer; I have seen your tears.
(2 Kings 20:1-7 NRSV)

Cancer, heart disease, diabetes, COPD (chronic obstructive pulmonary disease), accidents, asthma, and strokes—you don't have the last word! You may beat me up and slow me down; my body may have aches and pains that are unrelieved by over-the-counter and prescription medications, *but* my life is hidden with Christ! Jesus already won this battle for me! I am more than a conqueror!

Jesus, please hear my weak cry, too feeble to come through parched lips. Jesus, see my pain that has no end in sight. Jesus, your name is the only one I know that can soothe and calm my fears. Jesus, Jesus, Jesus! Come quickly!

We know our merciful God through Jesus Christ will be present at bedsides when we lie down but sleep doesn't come, death is outside the door, our spirits are uneasy and fidgety, and our eyes can't find rest. We believe the Holy Spirit will be present with those who are standing at the River Jordan preparing to cross over.

When our time on this earth is over, we are trusting and believing the Lord will be present to see us to our eternal rest. May we take comfort in our hearts each day that every prayer, every tear, and every sob are seen by our God. Grant us O' God another chance to fight—we pray.

We pray this prayer in faith and thanksgiving to the only wise God, our Savior, Jesus Christ. Amen!

1. As I am praying this prayer, I am remembering …

2. How am I being called to respond to this prayer?

3. What challenges me?

7

I give thanks to you with all my heart, Lord. I sing your praise before all other gods. I bow toward your holy temple and thank your name for your loyal love and faithfulness because you have made your name and word greater than everything else. On the day I cried out, you answered me. You encouraged me with inner strength. (Psalm 138:1–3 CEB)

Every day, O Lord, let this mouth of clay you have made and the lungs you have filled with life-giving oxygen praise you. Please let every shred of my being lift up your name and give thanks, for I love you with all my heart and soul! Let every act I commit, every thought I think or imagine, bring honor and glory to your great majesty!

In good times and bad, we will praise you. For family and for friends, we praise you! For the capacity to love and forgive and for the gift of the day, we praise you! For newborn babies and mended relationships and for healing the brokenness between parents and children and sisters and brothers, we praise you!

For the coming together of communities and cities and leaders and nations, we praise you!

When we look at snowcapped mountains and lush valley's we praise you! For the sound of birds early in the morning to awaken us to a new day, we praise you! For the chirping of crickets at dusk to signal the ending of another day of life, we praise you! For rain that waters and the sun that heats and dries, we praise you!

Praising you day and night fills our souls with joy! Even as we drift off to sleep and awaken early in the morning, our hearts are filled with praise for you. You are worthy of more praise than our feeble bodies can produce. Praise to you is worth more than anything we own or could purchase or possess. Praise to you fills our souls with overflowing joy.

Around your throne the angels are praising you day and night. Please accept our humble attempt to lift up your name and bless you this day for all you have done in our lives; for all you do each and every day, for all of us. Thank you.

1. As I am praying this prayer, I am remembering …

2. How am I being called to respond to this prayer?

3. What challenges me?

8

Forgiveness

When word of it reached the king of Nineveh, he got up from his throne, stripped himself of his robe, covered himself with mourning clothes, and sat in ashes. God saw what they were doing—that they had ceased their evil behavior. So, God stopped planning to destroy them, and he didn't do it. (Jonah 3:6–10 CEB)

Lord, when I look at all my mistakes, all the times you were with me and I ignored your presence, I see the mess I have made of my life! Help me to stop, fast for a season from things of the world, and concentrate on you and your presence in my life so I can follow you. Forgive me for all the times my rebellion was stronger than my witness. Forgive me when I didn't sit down and meditate on your word and call on your name. Forgive me when I didn't fall on my face, my knees, at your altar and cry out to you. Forgive me!

In spite of it all, all my falling down and getting up and falling down and getting up, I can still give thanks to you for forgiving me over and over again when I made a mess out of even simple things. Thank you for picking me up when I have fallen down and fallen short. Show us, loving God, the path you would have us to take. We have lost our way! Plant our feet on the solid rock of your Word.

Forgive us when we are silly, thinking we are wise in our own eyes. Forgiving and patient Jesus, forgive us, for we do not know what we are doing!

When we treat others as if we are better than they are because we have more than they do; more privilege, power and prestige, more education and know people "in high places." Healer, Way Maker Jesus, forgive us, for we know not what we do!

When we smugly sit with satisfaction on our faces because we have achieved the material things in life while some of our brothers and sisters struggle each day just to get by; struggle with self-esteem, struggle with addictions, struggle with mental health, struggle with rent and groceries, struggle with discrimination, Holy One, forgive us, for we do not know what we are doing!

When we go to our churches and find joy in being with people who are like us and do not take the gospel to those who are in need of healing and hope, who don't look like us, Strong High Tower, forgive us, for we do not know what we are doing!

When we throw pennies and pittance to those who need a relationship and a gentle and loving touch because we are too busy to get involved, God of strength and power, forgive us, for we do not know what we are doing!

Lord Jesus, help us! Heal us! Move within us!

This is our prayer as spoken to us in Psalm 103:10-14 (NRSV) He does not deal with us according to our sins, nor repay us according to our iniquities. For as the heavens are high above the earth, so great is his steadfast love toward those who fear him; as far as the east is from the west, so far he removes our transgressions from us. As a father has compassion for his children, so the LORD has compassion for those who fear him. For he knows how we were made; he remembers that we are dust.

In the awesome name of our Savior, Jesus Christ, who has mercy upon us. Amen!

1. As I am praying this prayer, I am remembering …

2. How am I being called to respond to this prayer?

3. What challenges me?

9

Courage

After Moses the Lord's servant died, the Lord spoke to Joshua, Nun's son. He had been Moses' helper. "My servant Moses is dead. Now get ready to cross over the Jordan with this entire people to the land that I am going to give to the Israelites. I am giving you every place where you set foot, exactly as I promised Moses. Your territory will stretch from the desert and the Lebanon as far as the great Euphrates River, including all Hittite land, up to the Mediterranean Sea on the west. No one will be able to stand up against you during your lifetime. I will be with you in the same way I was with Moses. I won't desert you or leave you. Be brave and strong, because you are the one who will help this people take possession of the land, which I pledged to give to their ancestors." (Joshua 1:1–6 CEB)

Gracious God, over and over again, my knees get wobbly, my heart races, my palms sweat, and my mouth is dry. I am afraid! What will others think if I make a mistake? What if I'm not hearing from you and it's my own imagination? I am nervous! Can I do it? Can I go where the Lord is sending me? Can I say with boldness and confidence the words the Lord has given me? Why am I so afraid? Get behind me Satan! Grant me dear Lord the courage of Joshua to go and lead your people in the way you direct me. Stand up in my spirit that I may always feel your presence. I know you have already gone before me and prepared the way. Everyplace you send me, you have already given. For that I am thankful.

When I am confused and don't know which way to turn, when I find the way but am afraid to go there, grant me courage as you did to Peter and John. I may not have attended the finest university in the land or have the most prestigious degree, but I do love you, Jesus! I believe you died for my sins and that I have been purchased with your blood. Because I love and trust you, help me to walk boldly in all that you have given me to do without fear and trepidation.

When things come my way and I don't think I have what it takes, remind me that you are with me and in me and that you work through me. Remind me that no weapon formed against me will prosper. Remind me that you will strengthen me, whisper to me, help me, hold me, and walk with me. Help me remember those who were simple fishermen inspired others with the boldness of Christ. Help us not to be afraid of whatever comes our way.

I will not fear in Jesus' name. Amen!

1. As I am praying this prayer, I am remembering …

2. How am I being called to respond to this prayer?

3. What challenges me?

10

Intercession

The men turned away and walked toward Sodom, but Abraham remained standing in front of the LORD. Abraham approached and said, "Will you really sweep away the innocent with the guilty? What if there are fifty innocent people in the city? Will you really sweep it away and not save the place for the sake of the fifty-innocent people in it? It's not like you to do this, killing the innocent with the guilty as if there were no difference. It's not like you! Will the judge of all the earth not act justly?"

The LORD said, "If I find fifty innocent people in the city of Sodom, I will save it because of them."

Abraham responded, "Since I've already decided to speak with my Lord, even though I'm just soil and ash, what if there are five fewer innocent people than fifty? Will you destroy the whole city over just five?"

The LORD said, "If I find forty-five there, I won't destroy it."

Once again Abraham spoke, "What if forty are there?"

The LORD said, "For the sake of forty, I will do nothing."

He said, "Don't be angry with me, my Lord, but let me speak. What if thirty are there?"

The LORD said, "I won't do it if I find thirty there."

Abraham said, "Since I've already decided to speak with my Lord, what if twenty are there?"

The LORD said, "I won't do it, for the sake of twenty."

Abraham said, "Don't be angry with me, my Lord, but let me speak just once more. What if there are ten?"

And the LORD said, "I will not destroy it because of those ten." When the LORD finished speaking with Abraham, he left; but Abraham stayed there in that place. (Genesis 18:22-33 CEB)

Gracious God, thank you for your grace and mercy in our lives. I ask, O God, that you would bless those we love and those you have entrusted to our care. Lord, you heard the prayer of Abraham as he interceded for the people of Sodom and Gomorrah, hear our prayer today. Lord God Almighty, you heard the prayer of your precious Son Jesus who interceded for his beloved disciples. Hear our prayer this day as we lift up those who fight for justice and righteousness around the world. Lord, we ask that you send angels to them and guard them in all their ways.

Lord, we stand in the gap for our children and families, neighbors and strangers who fight against evil and flee for their lives in conflicts and wars. Hear their prayers, O Lord, we ask. Hear the prayers of those who have been captured and are prisoners of war. Hear the prayers of those who suffer atrocious abuse at the hands of their captors. Hear the cries of hungry children whose bellies ache and their heads throb. Hear the cries of distraught parents whose children suffer from diseases of poverty and lack.

Hear our prayers, Lord God, in the name of Jesus! Protect and save your people! Give us the tools and the wherewithal to intercede not only with our prayers but with our resources. Help us to love one another as you have loved us. Hear the prayers of those who pray each day, day and night, for the welfare of others. Give us hearts of tender flesh to pray without ceasing. This day, O Lord, hear our prayers for our brothers and sisters who grieve, those who are lonely and alone; those whose self-esteem suffers; those dealing with depression, those who have paralyzing anxiety and fear; those who are bullied and terrorized, those who struggle with addictions ... Hear our prayers, O Lord!

1. As I am praying this prayer, I am remembering …

2. How am I being called to respond to this prayer?

3. What challenges me?

11

Supplication

> LORD, listen closely to me and answer me, because I am poor and in need… Listen closely to my prayer, LORD; pay close attention to the sound of my requests for mercy. Whenever I am in trouble, I cry out to you, because you will answer me. (Psalm 86:1, 6–7 CEB)

Lord God, our needs vary from day to day and sometimes from hour to hour. We get a phone call, a text, or a Facebook message, or someone comes to our door with news that knocks us to our knees. It takes our breath away. We can't wrap our minds around what we have just been told. Yet, we know you hear our prayers. Listen to us, O Lord Jesus, when we can't find words to pray, yet our souls are crying out with loud wails and screams. Guttural screams from deep within our bellies cry out in our pain, heart-wrenching screams that leave us weak and sometimes disoriented. When trouble comes upon us, hear our prayers, and come and see about us.

We know sometimes the news may come in the form of threats and intimidations. We know sometimes there are violent possibilities just because of who we are or what we believe. We realize and know within our hearts that you are the only one who can deliver us.

We do indeed believe we can do all things through our Lord Jesus Christ! We pour our hearts out to you this day to fill us with your Holy Spirit that we may speak to our circumstances and our situations with boldness, knowing whatever happens, you are with us!

When trouble comes knocking on our door, when fear comes creeping in our rooms, when the flood of tears won't stop, come see about us! Immerse us in the depth of your presence that we may feel your calm assurance and know beyond a shadow of doubt that there is no place we can go, where you are not already there.

1. As I am praying this prayer, I am remembering …

2. How am I being called to respond to this prayer?

3. What challenges me?

12

Fear

Don't fear, because I am with you; don't be afraid, for I am your God. I will strengthen you, I will surely help you; I will hold you with my righteous strong hand. (Isaiah 41:10 CEB)

Quickly! Come see about us, Lord Jesus! It is too much! The enemy of fear is so real. It's palpable! Fear is trying its best to consume my thoughts, to take over my mind. Don't let it!

All around me I see confusion, distrust, competition, and naysayers. Around me are those who would lift up their hands against me … if they could get away with it and protect their identity!

All around me are pitfalls, razor-sharp traps, and darkness. Oh, to be like a bird and fly far away and be at rest in your bosom!

As children need the quiet calm of a parent while crossing the street, so do I need you to hold my hand as together we walk victoriously in the midst of this battlefield. Though arrows or bullets may fly, I know you hold my hand. Though words like fire-torched darts may zoom past me, I will not be singed. Though traps have been set while the enemy hides in darkness, I know that darkness is like day to you, and they are visible to your naked eye. Because you are with me, I will not fear.

When there is confusion and chaos; when there is tumult and turmoil on the news and in the streets, I will not fear. When my knees tremble and my feet are unsteady, I will remember that you are holding my hand and will not let go. I will remember that there is no place I can go from your presence. I will remember that you are with me always, even to the ends of the earth. I will remember that I belong to you. I will remember that eye has not seen how you will uphold those you love. I will remember that your hand is always victorious. I will remember that you are indeed my Help! I will remember....

1. As I am praying this prayer, I am remembering …

2. How am I being called to respond to this prayer?

3. What challenges me?

13

But now more than ever the word about Jesus spread abroad; many crowds would gather to hear him and to be cured of their diseases. But he would withdraw to deserted places and pray. (Luke 5:15 NRSV)

Heal me in my quiet time with you.
Heal me of any disease that is brewing beneath the surface.
    Heal me of gluttony and gossip.
    Heal me of pride and powerful prejudice.
    Heal me of conceit and self-centeredness.
    Heal me of arrogance and narcissism.
    Heal me of my illusion of superiority.
    Heal me of my thoughts of inferiority.
    Heal me of my lack of unwavering faith.
    Heal me of false humility.
    Heal me.
    Heal.

1. As I am praying this prayer, I am remembering …

2. How am I being called to respond to this prayer?

3. What challenges me?

14

All of them deserted him and fled. A certain young man was following him, wearing nothing but a linen cloth. They caught hold of him, but he left the linen cloth and ran off naked. (Mark 14:50–51 NRSV)

My Lord Jesus, where were these healed people when you were deserted, tried, flogged and crucified? The authorities were always afraid of the crowd's reaction, and that fear kept them at bay. Where were they when you were on the Via Dolorosa? Where were they when you were mocked and spat upon? Where were those who were fed with the fish and bread who ate their fill with baskets of abundance left over? Where were those who brought their sick and laid them at your feet, and you healed them. Where were they?

Where are we when Jesus calls us after He has fed us and healed us of all our infirmities? Where are we when His forgiveness has been the fountain of life for us?

We know you were "the one" to be our sin offering, our sacrificial Lamb. We know you were born of a woman yet overcome in her womb by The Holy Spirit. We know the Father was always with you and that you did what your Father had determined centuries earlier would be done to save His people from their sins. We know that this same Jesus was raised from the dead on the third day with all power in His hands.

We too flee when we are afraid of the consequences of our actions and inactions! We too flee when we are ashamed of our apathy. We too flee when no one pursues because we are afraid to look in the mirror at what we have become.

What have I become?

Help me to stop running!

Lord, come to my rescue!

1. As I am praying this prayer, I am remembering …

   _____
   _____
   _____
   _____
   _____
   _____
   _____

2. How am I being called to respond to this prayer?

   _____
   _____
   _____
   _____
   _____
   _____
   _____

3. What challenges me?

   _____
   _____
   _____
   _____
   _____
   _____
   _____

15

How Long, Lord?

O Lord, who may abide in your tent? Who may dwell on your holy hill? Those who walk blamelessly, and do what is right, and speak the truth from their heart; who do not slander with their tongue, and do no evil to their friends, nor take up a reproach against their neighbors; in whose eyes the wicked are despised, but who honor those who fear the LORD; who stand by their oath even to their hurt. (Psalm 15:1–4 NRSV)

Lord, it has been so hard to listen and witness how we wound one another when it comes to politics! People who were once our friends are now our archenemies! Those we used to break bread with and sit with our feet under their tables are now distant memories.

We invoke your name as we go our way to do and say the things that lack any kind of glory to you! We say we are

Christians! It's a good thing we tell people because the evidence is not always there! We lie, mischaracterize, exaggerate, demonize, unfairly imprison, support unfair and unequal school systems, promote wealth inequality, and denigrate those made in your image! Help us!

We steal ideas, secrets, love and affection! We steal other's dignity, freedom, opportunities, rights, neighborhoods, educational, political and economic seats at the table. Our walk is not blameless.

We embellish, twist and turn upside down the truth.

We have killed our brothers' and sisters' dreams of a brighter future, a triumphant hope and confident spirit.

In our anger and hatred, we have physically and tragically killed those made in your image. We have hung them, stabbed them, shot them, knifed them, drowned them, beat them, run over them, and put our weight on their necks, hoping to destroy all they represent. In their death as in their life, you were with them when their last breath was taken.

Help us to stand, speak up and speak out and get in some good trouble even if we risk all.

1. As I am praying this prayer, I am remembering …

2. How am I being called to respond to this prayer?

3. What challenges me?

16

When in Trouble

> Save me, O God, for the waters have come up to my neck. I sink in the miry depths, where there is no foothold. I have come into the deep waters; the floods engulf me. (Psalm 69:1–3 NIV)

Almighty God, from whom there are no secrets (that means I can't hide a thing!), no desires that are concealed from your omniscience (so when I want to get back at my enemies, you already know), and who knows all our thoughts, even in the deep recesses of our unconscious (so you know even though it hasn't made it to my conscious awareness?)—O Lord, I need you to help me, for I am really in trouble!

I am running from my past mistakes. Running from thoughts that overwhelm my mind. I am racing to get ahead of the demons that chase me. I am jogging past the lies. I am outdistancing the abuse! Skipping past the deceit. I am racing toward the finish line of faith in a Savior who forgives all my sins and cleanses me from all unrighteousness! You know very well the weight of rebellious and wayward hearts.

I ask you, gracious God, to intercede on behalf of your child. I ask that you would be a Helper, Healer, Deliverer, and Strong Tower that she can run to and be comforted! Keep her safe and protect her. Bless those she loves.

Bless those who lift her up in prayer. Undergird her with your power and strength. Bind the evil one. Set warrior angels all around her. Let her rest in your peace. You have overcome the world on her behalf, and we are grateful knowing we could never repay you for your sacrifice. We thank you even now before the total manifestation has fully occurred. We believe you will complete what you have begun in us until your work is done. Work on me, Jesus!

It is in the mighty and matchless name of Jesus we pray. Amen!

1. As I am praying this prayer, I am remembering …

   _____
   _____
   _____
   _____
   _____
   _____
   _____

2. How am I being called to respond to this prayer?

   _____
   _____
   _____
   _____
   _____
   _____
   _____

3. What challenges me?

   _____
   _____
   _____
   _____
   _____
   _____
   _____

17

Praise

I will bless the LORD at all times; his praise shall continually be in my mouth. My soul makes its boast in the LORD; let the humble hear and be glad. O magnify the LORD with me, and let us exalt his name together. (Psalm 34:1–3 NRSV)

May the praise of our worship experience at home, in the church, in our car, at the park or in the shower this day usher us into the throne room of your grace. LORD, we bless you for your goodness and mercy that are unceasing. As we lift our voices in praise, let your Spirit come and fill this place.

LORD, we will boast of your healing to our souls and bodies all the days of our lives. Thank you for being present on foreign and national soil, hospital and hospice rooms, mean and diabolical streets, freak and frightful accidents, to save us so that we could give you the sacrifice of praise! You have given us an opportunity to ask, what would we have done if the LORD had not saved us?

We lift our voices to give thanks! Our hearts swell with joy at the sound of your name. Our eyes well over with tears as we think about what you have done in our lives. We thank you for prayers answered in ways we could not have dreamed or imagined. We thank you that when we didn't even know what we needed, you were already interceding and providing for us. Thank you!

Lord, if our feet start tapping, if we sway just a little bit with the music that's feeding our spirits and resonating in our souls, it's because we feel your presence deep down in the depths of our being. Saturate us in such a way that our lives are lived out joyfully in your presence.

1. As I am praying this prayer, I am remembering …

   _____
   _____
   _____
   _____
   _____
   _____
   _____
   _____

2. How am I being called to respond to this prayer?

   _____
   _____
   _____
   _____
   _____
   _____
   _____
   _____

3. What challenges me?

   _____
   _____
   _____
   _____
   _____
   _____
   _____
   _____
   _____

18

Prayers for Healing of a Child

> Then people brought little children to Jesus for him to place his hands on them and pray for them.. (Matthew 19:13 NIV)

Almighty God,
For this tiny, helpless little one, we ask for your merciful hand to touch this hurting helpless child, who, along with his parents, is in need of rest and assurance. We bring this child to you because of your great love for children. With all his being, he is crying out for relief. Disease and sickness, illness and injury tap all our resources. They leave us exhausted and, if we're honest, sometimes angry and frustrated.

You see the tears and pain of these parents. They have no one but you to turn to in this great hour of need. You are bigger than all these things: ventilators, CPAP, IVs meticulously placed in small feet or tender scalps, heart monitors, and multiple medications, x-rays, and ultrasounds. You can handle all our feelings and emotions. During this experience, let us grow closer to you.

Help us to hold on to your promises of never leaving us and being there when we call.

When you, Lord Jesus, laid your hands on those who had ears that could not hear or tongues that could not speak, you had mercy and touched them. We ask you to touch this child this night, in your name. Glorify yourself through a miracle on his behalf. We ask in faith, believing that all things are possible with you. In your mercy, sweet Lord Jesus, we ask. Amen!

1. As I am praying this prayer, I am remembering …

   _____
   _____
   _____
   _____
   _____
   _____

2. How am I being called to respond to this prayer?

   _____
   _____
   _____
   _____
   _____
   _____

3. What challenges me?

   _____
   _____
   _____
   _____
   _____
   _____

19

Morning Prayer

In the morning, while it was still very dark, he got up and went out to a deserted place, and there he prayed. (Mark 1:35 NRSV)

When I am clothed in darkness and the silence envelopes time, I look to you in the stillness and wait…
I fall into a restless sleep, waiting…
I awaken to a new day, listening…
I go about the day tarrying for the movement of the Spirit…
Please speak through us this day, that your people who hear us would hear a word specifically for their situation. If they need hope, encouragement, conviction, or peace in their souls, speak, Lord! We ask that those who are carrying heavy burdens will find them lightened as the day progresses. Speak Lord!

We pray that each of your beloved children will put down their weapons of war and hate, of dominance and subjugation, of power struggles and a need for personal glory. Speak Lord!

Help us to always humble ourselves before you. Help us to be a blessing to those where we have power to change circumstances.

Continue to strengthen us for the journey ahead. We are yours, body, mind, and spirit. Use us! Be glorified! Move us to act and think in ways that will change the world around us for the sake of the kingdom.

Speak Lord!

We ask all these things in Jesus's name. Amen!

1. As I am praying this prayer, I am remembering …

2. How am I being called to respond to this prayer?

3. What challenges me?

20

A Prayer for Those in Conflict

> Therefore, as God's chosen people, holy and dearly loved, clothe yourselves with compassion, kindness, humility, gentleness and patience. Bear with each other and forgive one another if any of you has a grievance against someone. Forgive as the Lord forgave you. And over all these virtues put on love, which binds them all together in perfect unity. (Colossians 3:12–14 NIV)

Lord, sometimes families struggle. Sometimes brothers and sisters are not speaking. Mothers and fathers are yelling at each other and swear they will never speak to each other again. Parents and children disagree on what's fair and just. Sometimes friends are doing things we don't agree with and make us uncomfortable.

Lord, sometimes we are confused! We don't know which way to turn. We don't know what to believe. We have lost what we thought was our moral compass. We are under spiritual attack. We know we're not in this alone. We need to feel your presence. How do we get our bearings? How do we function in this conflict? Does one person have to be right and the other person wrong? Where is the grace? Where is the mercy? Where is the forgiveness?

Help us get to a good place. Help us get to a place where we can see you. Help us love beyond our human capacity.

Where there is conflict in and between family members, heal, O Lord! Where there is conflict with governments and countries and factions, heal, O Lord! Where there is violence in the city and in the country, heal, O Lord! Where there is paralyzing fear of the unknown, heal, O Lord!

Heal the kind of unforgiveness that eats us up from the inside out.

Help us love with *your* definition of love, not ours. Help us to see others as *you* see them. We trust you to help us; no one else can. Thank you.

1. As I am praying this prayer, I am remembering …

   _____
   _____
   _____
   _____
   _____
   _____
   _____

2. How am I being called to respond to this prayer?

   _____
   _____
   _____
   _____
   _____
   _____
   _____

3. What challenges me?

   _____
   _____
   _____
   _____
   _____
   _____
   _____
   _____

21

When Life Is Difficult

> When you are disturbed, do not sin; ponder it on your beds, and be silent. (Psalm 4:4 NRSV)

Lord, I need help today! I am frustrated! I am angry! I am disappointed!

Please don't let me win in my anger! Please don't let me hold grudges in my heart!

Take away *anything* that separates me from your presence!

Do not let the enemy win!

Help me calmly talk out my challenges and disappointments.

Help me take a deep breath and *breathe*!

You know when a sparrow falls from the sky. You know how many hairs are on my head.

You know my struggles as I try to make sense of things.

I want to live holy! I want to think holy thoughts, but sometimes it's just beyond my capacity!

I'm taking a deep breath. I'm repeating scriptures, silently letting the words settle my spirit. Whew!

I can do it now.

I feel your presence turning down the heat.

Thank you!

1. As I am praying this prayer, I am remembering …

   _____
   _____
   _____
   _____
   _____
   _____
   _____

2. How am I being called to respond to this prayer?

   _____
   _____
   _____
   _____
   _____
   _____
   _____

3. What challenges me?

   _____
   _____
   _____
   _____
   _____
   _____
   _____
   _____

22

When Tragedy Strikes

Lord in your mercy,
Hear the prayers of your people at _____ Church and the prayers of their community. Please anoint the hearts and spirits of your people with the Balm of Gilead as they wrestle with the news about the disaster that has struck their town.

Help them deal with the blow that knocked the wind out of their sails. Please help this pastor and community of faith to continue to preach and pray your word. Please provide pastoral care for the church and the community. Let the prayers of the nation be the wind beneath their wings of faith. Remind each of us of your redemption and love that has so frequently been preached.

Now I ask you to help my sisters and brothers who have had so many tough issues to challenge them in their walk with you. Undergird each of them with your power and presence. Fill them with your Spirit, that they may run and not get weary, walk and not faint.

Grant each member a double portion of your anointing in these tough times, I pray through Jesus Christ our Lord. Amen!

1. As I am praying this prayer, I am remembering …

   _____
   _____
   _____
   _____
   _____
   _____
   _____

2. How am I being called to respond to this prayer?

   _____
   _____
   _____
   _____
   _____
   _____
   _____

3. What challenges me?

   _____
   _____
   _____
   _____
   _____
   _____
   _____
   _____

23

Sickness Does Not Have the Final Answer

> Heal me, O' LORD, and I shall be healed; save me, and I shall be saved; for you are my praise. (Jeremiah 17:14 NRSV)

Almighty God,
In you, holy and righteous one, all things are known—every single thing—and there are not any secret agendas or thoughts. We are praying for mercy.

I ask, O God, that you would reveal the cause and the cure for what your daughter or son is enduring. You made her/ him and are aware of every nerve, muscle, blood vessel, and brain cell. This is hard. This challenges, tires, and exhausts every reserve. Please give what is needed. I pray for *your* Spirit and power to align her/his body, mind and spirit with your perfect will. Heal him/her, and they shall be healed!

You are our Healer, our strong Tower, and our Deliverer from all hurt, harm, and danger. Be our Great Physician, and do a miraculous work in their life this day. Astonish doctors with recovery and strength. They will indeed glorify you for the gift of salvation and wholeness.

We give thanks in advance for the unparalleled love you have for us. It is in the mighty, sweet name of Jesus Christ we pray. Amen!

1. As I am praying this prayer, I am remembering …

2. How am I being called to respond to this prayer?

3. What challenges me?

24

Likewise the Spirit helps us in our weakness; for we do not know how to pray as we ought, but that very Spirit intercedes with sighs too deep for words ... No, in all these things we are more than conquerors through him who loved us. For I am convinced that neither death, nor life, nor angels, nor rulers, nor things present, nor things to come, nor powers, nor height, nor depth, nor anything else in all creation, will be able to separate us from the love of God in Christ Jesus our Lord. (Romans 8:26, 37–39 NRSV)

Lord Jesus,
There is nothing that can separate us from your love.
Neither cancer nor chemotherapy nor radiation nor surgery.
Neither nausea nor loss of appetite.
Neither tiredness nor weakness.
Neither balding, porta cath, nor pic line.
Neither infusion clinic nor multiple doctor visits.

No! None of these things will separate us from your merciful love!

As we wait for total healing, our trust is still in you. Though we don't understand, we still trust you. Continue to walk beside us so that we feel your nearness. Thank you for unimaginable love, which does not fade. We will wait on you until our change comes. We bless your holy name, sweet Lord Jesus, and give you thanks for this blessing of praise. Amen!

1. As I am praying this prayer, I am remembering …

2. How am I being called to respond to this prayer?

3. What challenges me?

25

I waited patiently for the LORD; he inclined to me and heard my cry. He drew me up from the desolate pit, out of the miry bog, and set my feet upon a rock, making my steps secure ... Be pleased, O LORD to deliver me; O LORD, make haste to help me. (Psalm 40:1-2, 13 NRSV)

Lord, we gather today in the sacred space of our hearts and minds, anxiously awaiting a word from the very throne room of heaven. Speak, Lord, for we are listening—not just with our ears, but with our hearts and spirits. Fill this inner sanctum of our being with your Spirit, and let the fire of your presence rest upon us! Help us to speak words of wisdom and knowledge for the good of the body of Christ.

We pray for those who struggle and are in need of a nonanxious presence.

We pray for those whose hearts are broken in grief yet again.

We pray for those who have lost the will to go any further.

We pray for those who have lost another battle, but not the war with addiction.

We pray for babies born addicted, crying high pitched cries, who cannot be comforted.

We pray for the woman who has left her abuser and has returned over and over again.

We pray for young children exploited on the streets.

We pray for those who are vulnerable to a virus that snatches life and strength.

We pray for those brutalized and murdered because they are Black, Asian, Women, Gay, because they are…….

Today we pray.

1. As I am praying this prayer, I am remembering …

   _____
   _____
   _____
   _____
   _____
   _____
   _____

2. How am I being called to respond to this prayer?

   _____
   _____
   _____
   _____
   _____
   _____
   _____

3. What challenges me?

   _____
   _____
   _____
   _____
   _____
   _____
   _____

26

As a deer longs for flowing streams, so my soul longs for you, O God. My soul thirsts for God, for the living God. When shall I come and behold the face of God? (Psalm 42:1–2 NRSV)

O Lord, you are my strength and song! You are the Lifter up of my head!

You are our Warrior who fights our battles!

You are the Great Physician who heals every sickness and disease!

You are our Help when the situation looks as though we have been defeated!

You are our Hope when others say it is over!

You are our Comforter in the midnight hour!

You are the Net to keep us from falling too far!

You are the Light when darkness overtakes us!

You are our Companion when friends forsake us!

You are the Calming Lavender in our soul diffuser!

You are Ice Water for a parched and dry soul!

You are …

1. As I am praying this prayer, I am remembering …

2. How am I being called to respond to this prayer?

3. What challenges me?

27

> The Lord is near to the brokenhearted, and saves the crushed in spirit. (Psalm 34:18 NRSV)

Gracious God, today we lift this family to you that needs no introduction. You know them because their works and their witness speak for them. The compassionate nature of their hearts is known to you. The praises and prayers they have lifted up over the years have come before you, time and time again. They need the comfort of the gracious Holy Spirit to console them.

They are grateful for the good years and the blessings you so graciously bestowed upon them. Thank you for the memories made and the laughter shared. Thank you that our lives are better because they lived. Come, Holy Spirit, come Heavenly Dove and make your presence known. We give you thanks for welcoming this (mother, father, sister, brother, child, aunt, uncle) into your loving arms. Grant eternal peace. We pray in faith in the name of the one who gives all good and perfect gifts. Amen.

1. As I am praying this prayer, I am remembering …

   _____
   _____
   _____
   _____
   _____
   _____
   _____

2. How am I being called to respond to this prayer?

   _____
   _____
   _____
   _____
   _____
   _____
   _____

3. What challenges me?

   _____
   _____
   _____
   _____
   _____
   _____
   _____

28

God is our refuge and strength, a very present help in trouble. Therefore we will not fear, though the earth should change, though the mountains shake in the heart of the sea; though its waters roar and foam, though the mountains tremble with its tumult ... Be still, and know that I am God! (Psalm 46:1–3, 10 NRSV)

O God, how excellent is your name in all the earth! The heavens declare your glory under the tent of your splendid presence! The earth's seas pound with a loud rhythmic staccato while the tops of mountain peaks rise in majesty to greet each dawn covered by the snowfall of heaven's overflow. You are great and magnificent, and your goodness and mercy to mere humans demonstrate the depths of your unfathomable love.

You have kept us and held on to us even when we felt we could not hold on any longer. You rescued us from ourselves and others who would harm us. Disease and sickness, pain and weariness have come knocking at our doors. We pray you would continue to place a hedge of healing and protection, hope and assurance around those of us who have struggled. There is no trouble, no crisis, no distress where you are not present. Help me to be still and wait on the troubling of the water or the overwhelming overpowering of your presence. Please hear our prayers, O Lord, and grant us your peace!

1. As I am praying this prayer, I am remembering …

2. How am I being called to respond to this prayer?

3. What challenges me?

29

I cry aloud to God, aloud to God, that he may hear me. In the day of my trouble I seek the Lord; in the night my hand is stretched out without wearying; my soul refuses to be comforted … You are the God who works wonders; you have displayed your might among the peoples. (Psalm 77:1-2, 14 NRSV)

Planner of promises, Counsel to the wise, Hearer and Answerer of prayers, Heart of the righteous, Forgiver of sins, and Healer of pain, we pause to give thanks to you, everlasting Father, almighty King of heaven and earth!

Thank you so much for your faithfulness toward us! As we begin each day anew, we give thanks for those you have given to us to lead us on the way of righteousness and peace.

Be with those whose lives are challenged by aging bodies, diseases, fragility, and cloudy minds. Give them comfort and pain-free days. For those whose spirits and hearts have been broken, refresh their souls with a fountain of joy that never runs dry. For those who grieve, comfort them in the deepest places of their sorrow. For those who are lost, use us to help them find their way to you.

Forgive us when we think our way is the only way. Help us reflect on your righteousness and hear your tender voice of instruction. Forgive us, I pray, when we miss the mark.

We are yours! Live within us, so much so that it is obvious that we belong to you!

1. As I am praying this prayer, I am remembering …

2. How am I being called to respond to this prayer?

3. What challenges me?

30

Heal me, O LORD, and I shall be healed; save me, and I shall be saved; for you are my praise ... The word that came to Jeremiah from the LORD: "Come, go down to the potter's house, and there I will let you hear my words." (Jeremiah 17:14, 18:1 NRSV)

Merciful Father, holy and loving Son, healing and forgiving Holy Spirit; we come this day with no fewer prayers of thanksgiving, praise, and petition. We come with empty buckets needing to be filled by the abundance of your love that it may overflow into a world that's grappling with a new normal.

Weapons of mass destruction are being found in homes across our county to kill and maim innocent people. We hear harsh words of hatred that try to overpower your message of goodness.

We see others as targets instead of your beloved. We dehumanize the ones you told us to welcome. We ignore those you told us were our neighbors. Have mercy on us, O God, and create in us clean, refreshing, and compassionate hearts.

Mold our hearts into hearts of clay so that the Great Potter of our souls can fashion us into tools worthy to help God's people live and not die and declare the glory of the Lord!

Speak to us, Our Father in heaven, so that our hearts are humble and pliable. Speak to us so that we might make amends to those we have injured. Help us love unconditionally, for all are made in your image.

Come, Holy Spirit, and dwell within us so that we may be comfort to those who grieve, hope to those who have lost their mooring, peace to those in mental anguish, and love to those who have no one.

Come, Lord Jesus! We welcome you!

1. As I am praying this prayer, I am remembering …

2. How am I being called to respond to this prayer?

3. What challenges me?

31

Bless the LORD, O my soul, and all that is within me, bless his holy name. Bless the LORD, O my soul, and do not forget all his benefits—who forgives all your iniquity, who heals all your diseases, who redeems your life from the Pit, who crowns you with steadfast love and mercy, who satisfies you with good as long as you live so that your youth is renewed like the eagle's. (Psalm 103:1–5 NRSV)

Oh, it's you again—cancer!
Almighty God, cancer has no power in your hands!
You healed leprosy, paralysis, blindness, and the inability to speak and hear, and you corrected spiritual disabilities! God, you raised Lazarus, and an only son for his mother, and a twelve-year-old little girl. We know that the same resurrection power that raised Jesus is still present today to raise us from sickness and even death, for I am a witness!
Please touch the body of your servant this day from the top of his head to the soles of his feet. Let CAT and PET scans

indicate a miracle has taken place. Let lab work show that cancer cells are no more! Restore strength and energy. Return the sparkle to dull eyes and the smile that has been missed.

You, O God, are a rewarder of those who diligently seek you. Please, as people who seek you with their entire being, hear all our prayers on behalf of your son this day. We give you thanks and are so grateful for your love.

We pray in faith in the name of Jesus. Amen!

1. As I am praying this prayer, I am remembering …

   _____
   _____
   _____
   _____
   _____
   _____
   _____

2. How am I being called to respond to this prayer?

   _____
   _____
   _____
   _____
   _____
   _____
   _____

3. What challenges me?

   _____
   _____
   _____
   _____
   _____
   _____
   _____

32

Seek the LORD and his strength; seek his presence continually. Remember the wonderful works he has done, his miracles, and the judgments he has uttered. (Psalm 105:4–5 NRSV)

Almighty God, we give thanks today for who you are: eternal, omnipotent, full of love, and abounding in grace! You are awesome and almighty! You are the Giver of life! We lift our eyes to you, O God, who make heaven your home and earth your footstool! We keep our eyes on you, the Granter of abundant mercy and the deep Well of forgiveness to all who call on your name. If it had not been for the Lord on our side, what in the world would we have done? We would not and could not make it on our own or in our own strength.

We ask you, Spirit of the Living God, to fall on us and drench us with your goodness! By your powerful Spirit we have a glimpse of who you are! We praise you for the anointing that breaks every yoke that attempts to bind us. You fill us and free us from the sins that so easily beset us. You are merciful and kind and supply all our needs in the pastures of your great love and deep streams of forgiveness.

We are your people, called by your name. You have heard our cries and paid attention to our prayers, and we are grateful. Hear us this day, O God, as your people are in need of you!

We lift to you those who are in need of comfort from pain, those discomforted by their circumstances, frequent illnesses, and weariness of heart and spirit. Some are saddened and in a state of anticipatory mourning; others are mourning the actual loss of loved ones.

Be with those who hunger and thirst for food not grown in fields. Be with those who thirst not for water that comes from a faucet. Be with those who long for peace, that is not found in substances.

Be with us.

1. As I am praying this prayer, I am remembering …

   _____
   _____
   _____
   _____
   _____
   _____
   _____

2. How am I being called to respond to this prayer?

   _____
   _____
   _____
   _____
   _____
   _____
   _____

3. What challenges me?

   _____
   _____
   _____
   _____
   _____
   _____
   _____

33

The Word became flesh and blood, and moved into the neighborhood. (John 1:14 MSG)

Light of glory, Power of love, Purveyor of grace, Forgiver of sins, Jesus Christ the righteous and Holy One, come and tabernacle within the deep recesses of our hearts and souls. Camp out, stay over, reside forever within us so that our lives will reflect the witness of your glorious presence. Alpha and Omega, come near to me! River of life, flow through me! Beginning and End, watch over me! Great I AM, speak to me! Bread of life, feed me! Son of God anoint me! Lamb of God, save me!

Gracious God, in our spirit, we bow on our faces before you! You are worthy of all our praise! We give ourselves away in your presence! We surrender; we are fully yours! Fill us, we pray, with wisdom, strength, health, and wholeness. Let your Spirit hover over us so that our will is lost in your will for us. Let our lives make a difference in the lives of those entrusted to our care, those we meet on the street, and those who have no friends.

Let your anointing within us flow into the world of hunger and despair, hopelessness and addictions. May your joy within us be incredibly contagious so that we pick each other up on the journey and walk hand in hand toward your kingdom.

We feast on your Word, the Light for all people, extinguishing the darkness around us. May grace and truth abide within our hearts as we pour ourselves out to those you have given us.

1. As I am praying this prayer, I am remembering …

2. How am I being called to respond to this prayer?

3. What challenges me?

34

Don't bargain with God. Be direct. Ask for what you need. This is not a cat-and-mouse, hide-and-seek game we're in. (Luke 11:10 MSG)

Lord, its praying time! When children are being bullied, feeling lost and alone; while children who are doing the bullying have no concept of the pain and wounds they are causing, the emotional scarring they are imprinting; the therapy and medications for anxiety and depression that may be needed to live through the brokenness. Too many young people are trying to find a way out—it's praying time!

When there is not enough money for groceries, when families have to decide between food and medicine, where there is not enough toilet paper or paper towels, spotty electricity because the bill at times isn't paid, when lunches are subsidized and churches give backpacks filled with school supplies to help children prepare for school so they will be able to master their subjects and not get behind and become part of the correctional system—it's praying time!

When young women secure rides from the airport or

a restaurant and never make it home and later their bodies are found; when human trafficking is becoming one of the largest industries in the country at the expense of children and migrants; when poverty in the wealthiest nation in the world is on full display; when millions of acres are burning in the west and the southern coast is being buffeted by one disastrous hurricane after another—it's praying time!

When Jesus prayed, demons came out, sickness and disease left people healthy and vibrant, people enjoyed the world's largest fish fry, bleeding ceased, and people were welcomed into the community.

Jesus, come and see about your people. Without you we just can't make it! Help us!

1. As I am praying this prayer, I am remembering ...

   _____
   _____
   _____
   _____
   _____
   _____
   _____
   _____

2. How am I being called to respond to this prayer?

   _____
   _____
   _____
   _____
   _____
   _____
   _____
   _____

3. What challenges me?

   _____
   _____
   _____
   _____
   _____
   _____
   _____
   _____
   _____

35

> I lift up my eyes to the hills—from where will my help come? My help comes from the LORD, who made heaven and earth … The LORD is your keeper; the LORD is your shade at your right hand. (Psalm 121:1-2, 5 NRSV)

Gracious God, for all those who watch and wait at hospital bedsides; for all those whom sleep has escaped because they don't know where their children are; for those who won't have enough to eat this Thanksgiving or Christmas; for those who will not find a present under the tree with their name on it; for those who won't know their employment status in the new year; for those who wear the uniform to protect us who won't hold their families and kiss their newborn babies; for those who are without shelter, who are consumed by substance abuse or suffer with mental health challenges; for all of those who are only known by you; have mercy upon them and drench them in your holy presence.

Though you sit enthroned upon the winged heavenly creatures, yet you turn your face from heaven and see the tears and pain of your people. You awaken the dawn and call forth the moon to shine at night, yet you turn your ear from heaven and hear our cries and petitions and see the anguish in our souls.

We rejoice in God our Savior! Restore to us a peace that passes all understanding. Hold us in the very palm of your hand. Heal our broken spirits. Pour salve into all our wounds. Wipe our tears. Calm our sobs.

1. As I am praying this prayer, I am remembering …

2. How am I being called to respond to this prayer?

3. What challenges me?

36

When I look at your heavens, the work of your fingers, the moon and the stars that you have established; what are human beings that you are mindful of them, mortals that you care for them? (Psalm 8:3-4 NRSV)

What are we, O God, that you would be mindful of us and show us your glory? We have sinned by thought, word and deed. We have left so many crucial things undone that you told us to do! We have neglected the poor and needy time and time again. We have not always listened to the cries of your people suffering from the lack of basic necessities. We have averted our eyes from those who dress in winter clothes in the middle of the summer. We shake our heads at those who eat out of garbage cans and go down the street talking to themselves and fighting invisible enemies. We have criticized "those people" because they just can't seem to get their lives together; falling into sin time and time again. Forgive us! We are saved by faith through your abundant grace!

1. As I am praying this prayer, I am remembering …

2. How am I being called to respond to this prayer?

3. What challenges me?

37

> For I am the LORD who heals you. (Exodus 15:26 NRSV)

For those who are sick among us, cool scorching fevers, alleviate the pain and discomfort of disease and illness, regulate irregular heartbeats, and lower blood sugars and blood pressures that are too high. Give doctors and nurses pause to reflect on your healing power as the sick miraculously recover. Let them be a witness that it was not by their power or might, but by your Spirit.

For those whose hearts are broken by the death of someone cherished, replace pain and sorrow with your gentle, abiding peace. For those whose tears won't stop flowing and whose sobs won't stop racking their bodies, hold them tight, dear Jesus.

Have mercy on us this day! Help us shed the robes of fear, disobedience, complacency, and neglect. Clothe us with your righteousness so that we may faithfully and lovingly follow you.

Through your Son, Jesus Christ our Lord.

Amen.

1. As I am praying this prayer, I am remembering …

   _____
   _____
   _____
   _____
   _____
   _____
   _____

2. How am I being called to respond to this prayer?

   _____
   _____
   _____
   _____
   _____
   _____
   _____

3. What challenges me?

   _____
   _____
   _____
   _____
   _____
   _____
   _____

38

> The heavens are telling the glory of God; and the firmament proclaims his handiwork ... There is no speech, nor are there words ... The law of the Lord is perfect, reviving the soul. (Psalm 19:1,3,7 NRSV)

O Lord, the heavens declare your glory, and the earth shouts your victory over all creation! Only your instructions are perfect, your laws faithful, your commands pure, and your judgments true and honorable. We worship you because you are good and holy! Your name is to be worshipped above all names on earth and in heaven.

You bring joy and gladness to our souls! You cause the sun to come out like a warrior and the moon as an armor bearer! You cause the earth to bow in wonder, praise, and adoration as your footstool! You are the God who is our Rock and Strength. You deliver us from our enemies, walk with us in our struggles, and comfort us in our distress. You strengthen us in our weakness, come to see about us in our loneliness and sadness, and empower us to trust when we can't see our way through. For all these things, we give thanks!

When conflict and violence, fear and frustration permeate our city and nation, help us see the goodness of your mercy, which overshadows the bad. We remember you are our God, and our soul thirsts for your presence, and our flesh faints for your power and glory to surround us.

When we have struggled to place one foot in front of the other, leaning on the loving and eternal arms of Jesus, we remember from where you have brought us and how you have kept us.

We wait and we rest and we hope in you!

Come, Holy Spirit!

1. As I am praying this prayer, I am remembering …

2. How am I being called to respond to this prayer?

3. What challenges me?

39

Have you entered into the springs of the sea, or walked in the recesses of the deep? ... Have you comprehended the expanse of the earth? ... Where is the way to the dwelling of light, and where is the place of darkness ... What is the way to the place where the light is distributed, or where the east wind is scattered upon the earth? (Job 38:16,18-19,24 NRSV)

Lord, you laid the foundations of the earth and determined its dimensions! Lord God, you dug the depths of the oceans and filled them with immeasurable billions and billions of cubic miles of water. You laid the cornerstone of the stars, knowing each one by name and location. You commanded the morning dawn to appear in the east, showing forth your glory. Lord, you know where light comes from and where darkness disappears. You give the east wind a home and lay out a path for the lightning! There is no one like you! We cannot begin to comprehend all that you are! Your compassions fail not and are brand spanking new each and every day of our lives!

For those who suffer at the hands and power of others, for those who hear words of condemnation that lack the grace of affirmation, for those who live in constant fear, for those whose bellies have never been full and for those who have never known peace, hear our prayers on behalf of those who may be nameless and faceless to us, but to you, O God, they are the apple of your eye and beloved children of the Almighty!

Thank you for touching those whose bodies hurt and whose strength is diminished and whose health is challenged.

Even when death comes creeping into our rooms, we are assured that when the trumpet blasts, we will be raised with a body that will not decay! Hallelujah! Thank God! Amen!

1. As I am praying this prayer, I am remembering …

   _____
   _____
   _____
   _____
   _____
   _____
   _____

2. How am I being called to respond to this prayer?

   _____
   _____
   _____
   _____
   _____
   _____
   _____

3. What challenges me?

   _____
   _____
   _____
   _____
   _____
   _____
   _____

40

"Greetings, favored one! The Lord is with you." … "For nothing will be impossible with God." Then Mary said, "Here am I, the servant of the Lord; let it be with me according to your word." Then the angel departed from her. (Luke 1:28, 37–38 NRSV)

We pause to remember a young girl who said, "Let it be with me according to your word." This Word became flesh and lived among us and came to save us from our sins and be our Emmanuel, God with us.

We remember during this Christmas season those who will be hungry the day after Christmas when their Christmas baskets are empty. There will be those still in the hospital and still on hospice who will need the presence of Emmanuel. There will still be those running and hiding, fearful and anguished who will need to experience Emmanuel. There will be thousands of children born to teen mothers who will not be born into welcoming environments with warm receiving blankets and parties celebrating their birth. They will need Emmanuel.

For those who make their homes under bridges and overpasses; for those who keep us safe as first responders; for those who rule and govern; for those who have no more bread, no clean water, or too little sanitation; and for those whose bellies have never known the fullness of a complete meal, we need Emmanuel, God with us!

For those in our own midst struggling with the flu and COVID and other respiratory infections, too sick to get out of bed and too weak to care for themselves, we need Emmanuel. For those who have been injured and for those who have been struggling with sickness for weeks and months, have mercy!

Help us to hold on until our change comes … until Emmanuel comes!

1. As I am praying this prayer, I am remembering …

2. How am I being called to respond to this prayer?

3. What challenges me?

Occasional Prayers

If you find yourself needing a quick text prayer,
maybe one of these will be a blessing.

NATIONAL DAY OF PRAYER

Gracious God, we cannot begin to imagine your great and glorious majesty! As we look out and see Your brilliant sky and feel the gentle cool breeze, we know the enjoyment these gifts are because of Your great mercy.

On this National Day of Prayer, we lift up all those in leadership positions. Please grant them wisdom beyond knowledge and skills. Please grant compassion, kindness, respect, generosity and integrity to all who lead. Please fill the hearts of those you have called with justice and mercy for all people.

You, O' God are our joy and delight! Protect us from all forms of evil that distress our spirits and our witness. Keep us safe from the fiery darts of the enemy that perpetuate poverty, injustice, hatred, confusion, lack of access to healthcare, inadequate and insufficient educational opportunities and the many factions that divide us. Forgive us when power, privilege, personality, and property are more important than Your people.

Help us to remember that whoever is kind to the poor, lends to the Lord. (Proverbs 19:17)

Help us to remember that when you were a stranger, we invited you in. (Matthew 25:31-40)

Remind us to not oppress foreigners, strangers, asylum seekers and migrants because we see that in You. (Exodus 22:21 and 22 23:6-9)

Help us to see all people as though we are looking into the face of God, since we are all made in your image. (Genesis 1:26)

Help us to not take advantage of or mistreat the widow, orphans, and the fatherless. (Exodus 22:22)

Help us to look out for the most vulnerable among us including those who are elderly, those who struggle with mental health challenges and those who never complete paying predatory lenders. (Exodus 22:25)

Help us to remember you are the Alpha and Omega, the Beginning and the End, the Root and Offspring of David and that you hold the keys to eternal life, death and hell. (Revelations 22:12-16)

Help us to remember to love the Lord our God with all our hearts, souls, mind and strength and our neighbor as ourselves. (Matthew 22:37-40)

Come, Lord Jesus, and help us to love. "This is how we know what love is: Jesus Christ laid down his life for us. And we ought to lay down our lives for our brothers and sisters. If anyone has material possessions and sees a brother or sister in need but has no pity on them, how can the love of God be in that person? Dear children, let us not love with words or speech but with actions and in truth." (I John 3:16-18)

We pray for all people, in all places, in all situations, and we pray in the Name of the Father, the Son and the Holy Spirit. Amen.

NURSES DAY PRAYER
We Remember

Physician of our souls, Healer of mind, body and spirit, Comforter in sorrow and Counselor in distress, we come to lift up all nurses today. You called them into a ministry of the vulnerable, the sick, and sometimes the hopeless and helpless.

On this day that has been set aside to recognize them:

We remember their many sacrifices of this past year….their families, friends, their losses, their own physical and mental health challenges…

We remember them not being able to go home and share a meal with their families, kiss their spouse or children good night or good morning…

We remember them having to strip in their garages before coming inside their homes, when they were able to get away safely…

We remember the hands of the dying they held close to their hearts.

We remember the prayers they prayed as some breathed their last.

We remember the valiant fight they fought for their own lives and sometimes lost.

We remember too often their tear-streaked faces and wet masks.

We remember the healthy and the feeble struggling to breath and the oxygen just wasn't enough.

We remember all the IV's, all the lines and all the monitors and all the stuff that just couldn't keep every fragile body functioning to its' full capacity...

We remember long days that stretched into long nights when the relief was too sick to come in...

We remember that God called nurses to be an extension of His loving grace and bountiful mercy.

This day O' God, bless every nurse with every spiritual blessing. Pour so much into their cups that they overflow. Crown their heads with goodness. Remember every prayer. Hold every tear. Anoint every kindness.

We pray in Jesus Name. Amen

And this is the boldness we have in him, that if we ask anything according to his will, he hears us. And if we know that he hears us in whatever we ask, we know that we have obtained the requests made of him. (1 John 5:14 NRSV)

Father, in the awesome and almighty name of Jesus Christ, the Anointed One, the Son of the living God, the one who is King of kings and Lord of lords, we come with thanksgiving and praise, for you are so worthy of all our praise. You are glorious! You are loving, kind, and generous. You love us unconditionally and forgive us over and over again. For all these things, we give thanks.

We bring before your awesome presence this day _____. You created him/her in your image. You breathed into him/her your breath and spirit. I ask with great humility for your power to heal her/his body. Prostate cancers/breast cancers/colon cancers are not too hard for you to heal. You created the heavens and the earth, the sea and all that is in them. You cast the sun and moon into the sky and know the location of every star. You know the depth and expanse of every ocean and galaxy. Please, Lord Jesus, touch them. Grant him/her wisdom and discernment to make wise decisions regarding their health. Put the right people and the best treatment modalities at their disposal. Let their body heal according to those things that are administered for your glory. Hear our prayer, O God, and grant it, we pray thee. We love you, Jesus, and give thanks to you. Amen!

May the God of all grace and mercy be your constant companion as you travel through and into the unknown. May his powerful presence soothe you, rock you, and carry you through your greatest challenges. May you get strength from his words, "I will never leave you or forsake you," and "Fear not, for I am with you!" May all the prayers of all those who love you flood your soul and be the wind beneath your wings. May you continue to be encouraged and filled by a hope that comes from faith. May you find rest and peace in your walk toward healing, wholeness, and health. You know and have made known the great deeds of the Lord in your life. Don't stop! Call upon the name of the Lord! Pursue God and his strength while seeking his face. Remember all the wonderful and might acts of God (Psalm 105:1-5 NRSV).

Dear _____,

May the God who created and formed you in your mother's womb destroy with vengeance the cancer cells found within your body. May the cooling presence of the Lord that was present in the cool of the day when the LORD walked through the Garden of Eden and things were whole—may that same wholeness permeate your body today. May you have peace that passes all understanding as you lie down and get up. May the glory of the Lord always surround and inundate your spirit and mind.

May you know that you know that God does indeed love you and that he cares that you would be in good health even as your soul prospers and thrives. May you know the love, admiration, and appreciation of family and friends. May you be filled with hope of a future with plans that God will prosper and not harm you. Then you can call upon the Lord and he will hear you and answer you. May this be so in the name of the Father, the Son, and the Holy Spirit! Amen!

> Why are you cast down, O my soul, and why are
> you disquieted within me? (Psalm 42:11 NRSV)

Don't give up! Help has already come! The everlasting God of all creation is with you, restoring you and making you new! It is God who gives wisdom to doctors and strength to medications. It is the Almighty who strengthens weak knees and feeble hearts. It is *God* who says it's not over; it's not done until he gives the final word! May the prayers of your family be a gentle prayer covering you today.

> I called on your name, O Lord, from the depths of the pit; you heard my plea, "Do not close your ear to my cry for help, but give me relief!" You came near when I called on you; you said, "Do not fear!" (Lamentations 3:55-57 NRSV)

God is with you! Do not fear or be in despair! Hope in the Lord who created you and placed his spirit in you! Be strong in the Lord and the power of his might as you fight the good fight of faith, encased in the whole armor of God! You are a mighty warrior, and you brandish a mean sword! Fight to the finish! Your family and friends fight with you!

Gracious Father,

You are great and greatly to be praised! You are our Light and Hope! You are our Provider and Healer! Thank you for being more than enough!

Your daughter is praising you in spite of her circumstances. Bless her with continued healing and strength. Grant a good appetite and little pep in her step! We bless you and give thanks to you for being so kind and tender with us. Thank you for a full recovery! Amen!

May the Lord God Almighty remove all sickness, disease, and illness from you and all those you love! May the Lord give you long life, excellent health, and a future with great promises! May the Lord your God grant your every heart's desire! May your heart, soul, and body be filled with the powerful sweet presence of the Holy Spirit overflowing and filling those around you. May you always know the love and grace of a compassionate and forgiving God. In the name of the Father, the Son, and the Holy Spirit!

Gracious God,
For the gift of _____, we give thanks! For his kindness and good heart; for his love of family and friends; we pray you would grant him a renewed sense of your healing power and holy presence! Grant him long life, health and strength. Hear every request made on his behalf. Breathe on him your breath of love. We love you, Jesus, and give thanks for your presence in our lives. Amen!

Gracious God,
Pour out your gracious Spirit, and touch _____'s body from the inside out! Cauterize bleeding vessels. Rehydrate his parched body. Give knowledge to those who care for him. Be

living Water! Be Healer and the great Physician of his soul, we pray in the name of Jesus Christ! Amen!

O' God, our Help, Hope, Strength, and Joy, you are the Great I AM! You are Sovereign! You create, lift high, see all, and bless us beyond imagination and worthiness! You heal frail bodies, encourage weak spirits, and anoint us for work beyond our physical and mental capacity!

Please honor our request for healing on this side of heaven. Your Son, Jesus, opened the eyes of the blind, healed those broken by paralysis and bleeding, miraculously alleviated fevers, and unstopped ears that could not hear the sweet melody of early morning birds singing. You moved tongues that could not lift their voices in praise and gave them a new way to talk. You are the same yesterday, today, and forever and you do not change. Through the power of your glorious Holy Spirit, overwhelm _____ with total and complete healing. We pray in faith in the name of the one who is Healer, Savior, and Hope, Jesus Christ. Amen!

Gracious Father, Son, and Holy Spirit, we come in prayer and thanksgiving, in praise and worship, in obedience and reconciliation. We come with deep contrition and heartfelt sorrow over our sins and wickedness which we commit each day by thought, word, or deed. We come with hearts overflowing with gratefulness for the overwhelming gift of your forgiveness and mercy. We come empty and broken yet determined by the Word that reminds us that when we are calling, you are answering; you let us know that you are here with us! Glory!

So we come with great humility of heart asking for healing and restoration. We lay all those we love at the foot of the cross, that the blood of Jesus might drop on each of them and cleanse and restore their bodies of cancer, heart disease, diabetes, depression, fear, anxiety, and COVID-19. We will not give these things dominion over the power of your Word or the water and blood that ran down that old rugged tree. Save, heal, protect, refresh, encourage, and fill with hope all your people who fight the same battle. Strengthen their resolve. Let them be witnesses of your grace. We pray in thanksgiving in the name of the Father, the Son, and the Holy Spirit. Amen!

Merciful Father, we give thanks to you for restoring our health and healing our wounds, injuries and sickness! We give thanks for renewed strength, endurance, tenacity, and hope for the journey ahead. We bless you, for all you have done is good and very good! Hallelujah! Inhabit our praise as we give ourselves to you this day. Have your way, and glorify your name in this place. Grant your people a double portion of the anointing that we might overflow into the world making a kingdom difference. In the mighty, awesome name of Jesus Christ we pray. Amen!

Almighty God, pour out your tender sweet Spirit on your waiting child every day. Heal joints, muscles, and nerves. Heal inside organs and tissues that have been touched by disease. Give assurance in her mind and spirit that you are present no matter the result. Decrease pain to the point it becomes nonexistent. Grant relief so rest can come. Give refreshing so restoration may happen at the depth of the soul. Let the prayers of families and friends and congregations and coworkers be wind beneath wings of hope to uplift your servant and precious child. Grant exceeding favor for faithfulness to the gospel and a lifetime of excellence in all areas. Fill her cup until it overflows with every gift and grace. We thank you now for your promises to hear us before we call and answer while we are speaking. We give thanks through Jesus Christ our Lord!

Lord Jesus, in your mercy! Cool feverish temperatures, I pray. Thank you, Lord Jesus, for being the great Physician! Let the medication work according to the way it was created and administered. Help take away pain, and give comfort. Thank you, Lord, for hospital physicians, technicians and nurses. Bless those who deliver the trays and empty the trash cans. Hear the prayers of all those who are lifting up your child this day. Please bring peace and comfort for a good night's sleep. We pray for spouse and children; siblings and parents and ask that you bring them comfort in this very challenging time. We ask in Jesus's name. Amen.

Grace and peace of the Lord Jesus Christ be with you!
I pray you and your sweet family are in excellent health

and that your souls are prospering in the transforming Word of God!

I pray God is answering your every prayer and healing every area that needs to be made whole. I pray that God would honor you and lift you up always. I pray that every matter that presents challenge and frustration would become a distant memory that you overcome with the power and presence of the Holy Spirit! I pray for your peace that will flow like a gentle flowing brook to an oasis of joy! May your heart soar and your spirit flourish. May blessings overflow your cup this day in the name of Jesus. Amen!

MOTHER'S DAY PRAYER

Gracious God, we give you thanks and praise for mothers today…

For those who bore children who were the delight of their eyes…

For those who gave their children up for adoption…

For those who lost their child before they took their first breath…

For those whose children lived only a few hours, a few days or a few months…

For those who did not know how to mother, nurture or love their children…

For those who struggle to feed and provide for their children…

For those whose children were stolen from them…

For those who lost their children to disease, accidents or trauma…

For those who did not want their children…

For those who mothered others though they never physically gave birth themselves…

For neighbors, and grandmothers and aunts and cousins and friends who became a village of mothers for every child needing discipline, love and attention…

For mothers who are no longer with us and have joined that great cloud of witness, we thank you for the gift of life given to us and the precious memories we cherish because they lived…

Gracious God, please bless mothers this day as we pay them homage for love well done! For those who struggle, encourage. For those who are overwhelmed, give peace. For those who are joyful, let it overflow.

Thank you for this precious gift we celebrate today. Pour the waters of baptism and grace over each of them that renews, refreshes and strengthens them for the journey.

We give thanks in Jesus Name. Amen.

When Death Is Imminent

Almighty God, pour out your Spirit on this family. They have loved, and adored _____ and trusted and appreciated his/her wisdom and strength all their lives. Put their hearts back together in their pain. Comfort them as they anticipate death of the one they love. Strengthen them and prop them up on every leaning and tottering side. Lord Jesus, we come! We come with thanksgiving and praise for his/her _____ years. We come heartbroken because of this life-threatening illness. We come in faith knowing that absolutely nothing can separate us from your love; neither pandemics nor fear nor lack, nor strokes or heart attacks or even death! You created us in your image and breathed into us the breath of life which has kept and strengthened _____ for these _____ years. You promised you would never leave us or forsake us, even and especially in our time of need. Come journey with him/her when the time comes and he/she closes their eyes in eternal rest. We are grateful there is no fear in God's presence. Hold our hand at the crossing of the Jordan into freedom land, a place where there is no sadness, sorrow, or tears. Into your hands, most merciful God, we release your son/daughter to your loving care. In the name of the Father, the Son, and the Holy Spirit. Amen.

Easter Sunday morning!
He is risen!
The grave is empty!
The tomb couldn't hold him!
Death couldn't defeat him! He lives!
And because he lives, we will live eternally with him! Hallelujah!
Let your hearts shout with joy! May the Spirit of the living God fill you!
Let the one who is thirsty come!
Let the one who wants eternal life as a gift come!

Salvation can be found in none other!

No other name has been given among all humanity through which we can be saved! Hallelujah!

Has he appeared to you lately?

Glory to the Father, the Son, and the Holy Spirit! Amen!

Surgery

Gracious and loving God, we come in the awesome and almighty name of Jesus who is the Christ. We come in the name of the one who is the great Physician and Captain of our souls. We come in great humility and thanksgiving for the abundance of your grace and mercy in our lives. We come knowing that there is nothing too hard for you to do. We come standing on the Word, which was made flesh and dwelled among us. We come in the name above all names where every knee will bow and every tongue will confess. We come laying our all on the altar of healing and wholeness. The altar where the sick can be made well. The woman with the issue of blood touched the hem of your garment. Drop down your garment from heaven this day that _____ might take hold and feel the anointing flow through her/him. Today, we come lifting up my friend, my dear, sweet friend. You created her/him in your image and know every muscle and fiber in her/his being. O gracious God, when there has been distress in her/his body, mind, or spirit, you remind us to fear not! You have given us life and abundance. Touch _____ today and make her/him whole. Be with the physicians, and give them additional skills and knowledge for her/his good. Let them bring back a good report from her/his surgical procedure. Give their spouse _____ a peace and calm that passes all understanding. Grant them the power of your glorious presence this day so that their hearts will be at peace. We ask this in the name of your Son, our Savior, Jesus Christ. Amen.

For a Death

May the God who created us and blessed us with long life, health, and strength, welcome us in our time of death into his glorious presence and the presence of the company of that great cloud of witnesses. We thank you, O God, for Jesus who knew our grief and sorrows and who died and rose for our sakes and sits at your right hand. Lord, you gave _____ to us, and now with heavy hearts and weeping spirits, we give him/her back to you to live and reign with you forever. Blessed be the name of the Lord.

Benediction

To the all wise and glorious God our Creator, the loving and forgiving Son our Redeemer, Jesus Christ, and the life giving and life affirming ever present, Holy Spirit, we give all this to you. We pray the blessings of your Presence on all who read, pray and meditate on these words.

Come alive in their souls Lord Jesus we pray.

For your honor and glory, now and forever more. Amen

Printed in the United States
by Baker & Taylor Publisher Services